# Dancing on a Rock

## Chrys Salt

**Indigo Dreams Publishing**

First Edition: Dancing on a Rock
First published in Great Britain in 2015 by:
Indigo Dreams Publishing
24, Forest Houses
Cookworthy Moor
Halwill
Beaworthy
Devon
EX21 5UU

www.indigodreams.co.uk

ISBN 978-1-909357-69-3

British Library Cataloguing in Publication Data. A CIP record
for this book can be obtained from the British Library.

Designed and typeset in Palatino Linotype by Indigo Dreams.
Author photograph by Sara Bain
Cover design by Ronnie Goodyer at Indigo Dreams
Printed and bound in Great Britain by 4edge Ltd.
www.4edge.co.uk.
Papers used by Indigo Dreams are recyclable products made
from wood grown in sustainable forests following the guidance
of the Forest Stewardship Council.

For Richard

# Acknowledgements

A huge thanks to all those who have offered advice and criticism during the writing of these poems – Donald Adamson, Elspeth Brown, Stewart Conn, John Harrison, and Tom Pow, all of whom have been so generous with their time. Most especially Donald Adamson, whose support and insights have been invaluable. My book is better for their input. All its imperfections are mine. Thanks also to Ghareeb Iskander for permission to publish his Arabic translation of The Insurrection of Poetry and to Ronnie and Dawn of Indigo Dreams Publishing who give their writers such support, understanding and benign midwifery. Last, but certainly not least, thanks to Creative Scotland for the timely writing bursary which enabled me to take a dedicated month in France to refine the collection.

ALBA | CHRUTHACHAIL

**Also by Chrys Salt**

Poetry collections:
*Inside Out* (Autolycus Press, 1989)
*Greedy for Mulberries* (Markings, 2009)
*Grass* (Indigo Dreams Publishing, 2012)

Pamphlet collections:
*Daffodils at Christmas* (The Galloway Poets Series, 1998)
*Old Times* (Roncadora Press, 2009)
*Home Front/Front Line* (Roncadora Press, 2013)
*Weaver of Grass/A'fighe le feur* (Hattericks House, 2013)

Books include:
*Here We Go – Women's Memories of the 1984/85 Miners Strike* (CRS) National Media Award
*We Are of One Blood* (The Woodcraft Folk)
*Of Whole Heart Cometh Hope* (Age Exchange)
*College Lives* (London University Press)
*Make Acting Work* (Methuen Drama UK and US)

www.chryssalt.com for more information on Chrys's writing credits and other work.

# CONTENTS

## listen

## Lost, longed-for, unexplained

## Ötzi: the Iceman

# Dancing on a Rock

For Ann
with

listen

**listen**

can you hear the fishes sing
clicking mandibles of ants
the slow sad slur
of snail trails over paths
and terraces
the fraying edge of daffodils
as Spring wears out
the falling shadow of a rose
silence of leaves
holding their Autumn breath
slipping geometries
of snow on stones

the planet
turning round and round
and years that slip like silk
through wedding rings

without a sound?

## Her surprise

"I'll creep inside her when she sleeps,
nymph in her cuckoo spit,
slip the latch of dreams,
focus her eyes on specificities —
pollen caught on furry legs of bees,
feathers' zip, intricacies of moss
and leaf, the flutter of their fall.
Her chinks and pains I will employ,
make out of words unsaid
my mystery. And when she wakes
hair, hands and table-top will glitter
with my spoor. Be her surprise!"

## Be like Icarus

flaunt joy,
swerve on cumulus
graze on wind's
pastureland
taste light
dress up in risky feathers
rest on the altar of the sun
oh it is worth melt
flame and falling
to be flight and song
above the maze
where you retrace yourself
see only where you've been

far

    far

        below


the hindering walls

# Lost, longed-for, unexplained

# Roots

Small, pigeon toed,
and buck-toothed as a donkey,
my parents thought I didn't stand a chance,
my Brummie accent the last straw.

*How now brown cow,*
*how now brown cow,*
the mantra of my youth
as Mrs Sadler
rounded my vowels,
tightened my consonants
with elocution.

*How now brown cow,*
*how now brown cow.*
Over and over.
*Do you remember an Inn,*
*Miranda?*
*Do you remember an Inn?*
*Dirty British coaster with its salt-caked smoke stack.*
*Do you remember an Inn?*

Now with my accent polished 'Radio 4',
Quinquireme of Nineveh from distant la-de-da,
rowing home to haven at the BBC
with a cargo of cut glass, apes and plums,
I miss that Brummie coaster with its salt-caked
smoke stack

butting down the channel
of those long-gone days
with its cargo of 'our kid', 'pikelets', 'lamping',
'tarar a bit', 'blarting'
round and round the Wrekin
and back to me.

Brummie slang: *our kid* – my brother/sister, *pikelet* – crumpet, *tarar a bit* – goodbye for a while, *blarting* – crying, *round the Wrekin* – taking the long way round, a serious detour.

*How now brown cow* – a mantra used in elocution teaching to demonstrate 'Queen's English' vowel sounds. *Do you remember an Inn Miranda* (from Tarantella by Hilaire Belloc), *Dirty British Coaster and Quinquireme of Nineveh* (from Cargoes by John Masefield) – both poems were used in elocution as memory exercises and to sharpen consonants.

## Albums

A post war wedding, mum's hair in victory rolls.
Chubby me held proudly on our patch of lawn.
Dad waving from a camper van in Russia.
All of us grinning to camera on holiday.
Me, with dreadful ringlets on a donkey.
Measures of life short as a click
on a mocked up smile.

None of mum in the big chair near the end,
lids flickering over rheumy eyes,
hair, chin bristles old dog wiry. Slack
jaw agape, throat gargling mucus snores.

...because it isn't as if anything captures anything,
not the grit in our white bread sandwiches,
or being a widow longer than a wife.

...because before it or after it is rationing, or grief,
a blow-out on a foreign road,
mum driven to her nature's end
by me screaming with colic,
hating my braces, endless trips to the orthodontist
the rags dad tied in my hair to stop it frizzing,
tufting carpet from old cardigans,
not enough money for shoes, school uniform,
the gas bill, anything.

…because later, she would wake up with a smile,
ask flirtatiously 'might there be tea?'

…because some things are better left un-photographed
so only what seems the best of it remains.

## Soonest mended

I was shooed from rooms,
waited long hours on the bottom stair
straining for clues.

Cups ferried past and slopped on trays.
Words hissed like gas behind the front room door.
Aunt Win, who looked as if she knew a thing or two,
plied me with orange juice and pulled a face.

When they came out,
the Rich One, Uncle George,
bent down, slipped me a ten bob note,
winked with his crooked watery eye,
muttered 'least said.'

Scuffed shoes scuttled down the hall,
varicose legs in Lyle, smell of cheap talc,
then Players No 10 and Brylcreem slick
went out with dad,

me on the stairs,
frightened, small,
blood blooming from a bitten quick.

# My Top of the Pops (i.m. FAS)

With Bill Hayley I rocked,
rocked around the clock
with my partner in jive,
my top of the pops.
Gave it wellie.

Net petticoats swirled
as I rattled and rolled,
boogied and bopped,
hip-bumped and dropped,
wiggled and jiggled
my belly.

Not 'Salty' or 'Titch'
to the grammar school bitch
who thought cruel nicknames
were funny.
My dad was Bill Hayley
and I was his chick
so cool, so alive
in my brand-new tits,
in the groove with the moves
of the kids
on the black and white telly.

# Dirty Work

Dad's chickens were Rhode Island Reds
he'd reared from chicks,
all strut, duck, cluck and gossip,
red combs flopping, yellow feet
stretched to wizened octaves
as they scratched in the dirt for bugs.
They all had names,
ate just about everything,
scavenged for leftovers
like refugees on rubbish tips.
Greens, pumpkin, mashed potato,
half-chewed sausage, anything.
I loved the way they bobbed and tilted
in a beady sideways dance,
beaks quick as the needle of mum's Singer.
Once they were good and fat
dad screwed a humane poultry killer
on the fence, said it was painless, quick.
Caught Betty, put her neck into the guillotine.
We heard it snap.

Head hanging off she flapped
and staggered round the yard,
a ghastly pantomime of being alive,
not dying for what seemed
a long, long time.

Dad couldn't look us in the eye.
My brother cried.
Mum tried to hold her quiet
until she died.

We buried Betty in the flower bed,
her passing marked with a memorial rose.

Then ate a shop-bought chicken for our Sunday roast.

## Good neighbour

Our neighbour built big bonfires for us
on the allotment behind our house.
Stoked it with chestnuts, told us where
hibernating toads and slow worms were.
Left little messages, pipe cleaner men,
surprises in the doorway of our den.
Found us an orange box to make a table.
He made my childhood memorable.
One evening sitting on his knee
watching Tom and Jerry on TV,
his hand crept slyly up my frock.
tickly at first, then confusion, shock
wrong mixed with right, stock-stillness, fear,
senses uncharted, half of me not there.
His fingers pushed inside me, nothing said
as Tom chased Jerry round and round my head.
He told me not to tell. I never did,
but next time he called round I hid.
Had a knack with kids our next door neighbour.
I wish I'd told my mum about John Bridger.

Pipe-cleaner men – fibre-covered wires used to clean a tobacco
pipe were bent into shapes to create little characters.

## 20/20 Vision

The leather case that held her
buckled body straight
was hard to hug.
It swung between two sticks,
iron braced legs lugged after it.
What if she fell I'd speculate,
would she be like my tortoise
on its back, arms and legs awaggle?
Or when she took it off,
bend like an anglepoise,
slump like my knitted dolly
in the middle?

Words in my young head –
Polio. Spastic. Cripple.

Aunt Kath wasn't a real aunt,
but Mum's 'best friend' from school,
part of childhood's furniture.
I preferred her to the boring bunch
who called on us for Sunday lunch,
talked about haberdashery,
but never talked to me.

Kath had a car, her own optician's shop.
From time to time she'd check my eyes
with tests I'd try to memorise:

# I WANT TO HAVE
## GOOD EYES
### I SIT NEAR
#### GOOD LIGHT
##### WHEN
###### I
###### READ

She made my eye-tests fun,
always came up with a different one
to those I had remembered, but outgrown.

# E

# LV

## ISA

### ARON

#### PRESL

##### EYTHE

###### KINGOFROCKANDROLL

Kath had no children of her own,
none to bequeath her of gifts of blood.
To me she left a new vocabulary

# GRO

# WNFROMTHEGRI

## TINSIDEHERSHE

### LLAPEARLOF SOMETHINGB

#### ETTERUN

##### DERSTOOD

## In Retrospect (for DC)

Chatting on the sofa you and me,
you told me a friend's kitchen was fifteen years old.
You couldn't believe it.
The life of the kitchen.
The time between her arrival and divorce.
It had gone by in a blink you said.
Fifteen years, and what had you done with it?
You told me that given your genetic history
you probably only had fifteen years left.
And you began to cry.
I trotted out platitudes about a red chair
I'd reupholstered being there after me –
and minding that.
About there being no going back,
no way to reinvent the couch potato days,
no point in wishing things otherwise.
As if children, friendship, work and love
weren't enough to make sense of it.

And I asked you,
starting from now, what would you do
to make what's left of it worthwhile?

And you said you had started tai chi,
that it made you forget
the before it and after it
the losses you couldn't fix.

And I said I liked dancing.
Should we go?
And you said, and I said,
and you said, and I said
and we laughed
on the sofa you and me.

## Photograph of chairs (for HB)

One is wicker, waterlogged with rain,
the other a dining chair – left out
as if a ceremony's about to start.

Drifts of leaves have gathered round the legs.
Seats are sagging with a weight of loss.
Behind, arches and columns of a silent copse.

Chairs where we might have sat
had things been otherwise.
Found a quiet spot like this to read and chat.

You in the dining chair perhaps,
refocusing your camera,
me scribbling poems in the wicker one.

You drank yourself to death at forty two.
I live on with husband, children, love –
your photograph of chairs.

## Toad march

Leaving potatoes on the hob to boil
we ventured out in Macs and wellies
down the puddled track.

The light had gone.
Leaf mould and mud hissed under us
like nests of snakes,
then in a globe of torch,
we saw we stood up to our ankles
in a sea of toads.
Behind us, round us, under us,
seething and numberless
they clambered over rut and boot
croaking in warty congress
on each other's backs,
jewelled eyes
focused with single purpose
on their breeding ground.

*'What did it matter if we trampled some,*
*crushed their tiny lives into the leaves?*
*There would be other toads*
*other journeys such as these.'*

Yet we stood still as trees,
fearing to cause the smallest injury.
Wondered how many we had trodden on,
if the potatoes had boiled dry?

## Reflection

I am being stalked by a little old lady.
I glimpse her in shop windows,
the chrome of car headlights,
my bedroom mirror.
But she is too quick for me.
I turn my head
and she disappears
only to reappear in picture glass,
a polished table top,
the television screen.

Down at the station
The police think I've gone barmy

strange

because she was evident in the constable's bifocals
as he reluctantly took a note of my visit.

## Firing her up

When new, she awoke with the starter,
sprang like a leopard on ignition.
It was Brands Hatch, high velocity,
fuelled with testosterone,
pistons going like the clappers,
a crescendo of revs
hungry to reach their destination.
Tyres, everything screaming,
then a slow breaking,
an exhalation of exhaust,
a coming to rest like quiet breathing.

Now he uses a crank handle to get the old girl started,
a careful nurturing of clutch and gear.
He takes her out on quiet residential roads.
Although the electrics are not what they were,
the fine upholstery scuffed and lumpy,
he can still fire her up, he still loves her,
and given the right encouragement,
she still goes!

## Love on the beach

He must have been eighty,
she was topless, a dug
slung like a used condom
on his snowdrift of chest hair.
Skin slack as an elephant's,
hammocks of it drooping
under belly, forearm, chin,
this on a beach sprawling
with taut flesh, plumped,
oiled, sun bronzed, young.

And they were kissing!
Not a cheek peck, but full-on,
a lover's kiss,
tongues licking pleasure
from each other's mouths
(oblivious to disgust
and sidelong glance).

Let that be us I thought,
not daytime TV,
watching amaryllis grow,
pullovers with v-necks
from catalogues,
crosswords and puzzle books,
small dreams, string vests, big pants
and running out of talk.

But bite and suck and roving hand,
still lovely to each other
on the sultry sand.

## A Burns Supper (for JBP)

He leaves a tantalising tit-bit hanging
for our imaginations to elaborate.
Loses the ends of things,
searches the house inside his head
room after room,
but can't remember when he had them last
or put his hands on them.
His sorties into memory come back with shards
of loveliness he can't reconstitute,
the past a country seen through gauze
as shadowland.

So it is.

Sometimes she who has loved him
all their married days,
fills in a clue
to make sense of him.

Today we take him a Burns supper,
tatties, neaps, haggis
in a heated bag.
He enjoys what he can,
but can't finish it.

Tastes he's lost the names for
linger on his tongue.

## All my friends (for JBP)

'All my friends...'
A question mark tries to hook the end of it.
Yes? All your friends are...?
Always a mistake to hurry him.
'All my friends are...'

Down the vortex of lost memory
a shiny fish-tail vanishes.

Then, triumphantly he lands it.
'All my friends are dead
or in prison.'

He stares out through the bars.

## Road test

they take blood
test lung function
X-ray the pulsing caves
where breath and blood
pass secret messages
and heart
beats back its Morse
in bulletins
of coded information
how long my track
of days
how far
the destination?

## Freeze-frame

As if she'd overwound the clock
un-seamed the hours
between a tick and tock
on a last syllable
of having been
a breath half in
and half way through
the way leaves snap free
or the proboscis of a bee
freeze-frames on the lost names
of flowers
when a word
on the arched tongue
unsays the names of birds
or something precious slips
and hangs half-way between
itself and smithereens.
As if she'd overwound the clock
somewhere between a tick and tock

## Birdsong

Before it was the last time of seeing,
that slip between falling and dying,
head split open on the sink
mouth unhinged in foothills of alarm,
hands fast-framed to starfish.
Before blood seamed geometries of tiles
rust stain, soap smear, and silverfish.
Before she knew the underside of things
she heard a voice like birdsong
saying 'It is Made.'

## Blackbird (i.m. JWS)

A blackbird got into the kitchen yesterday,
flew at the window,
dropped to the breadboard,
flew back with certain aim at dark cloud
broiling beyond the pane.
Perplexed, perhaps, that sky should be so solid,
it flew at it again, head butting space,
buddleias, the intransigence of rain.

I chased it round and round
until flustered with fright
it settled on mum's chair
(empty now for a year)
flimsy breastbone heaving
as hers used to do.
I homed in stealthily to capture it,
or shepherd it to the door,
but with a squawk
it found its own way out,
winged skyward,
radiant with liberty,
inhaling light.

# Inheritance

Cutlery, nicotined with tarnish
boxed on powdery cheeks of velvet.

Napkin rings in tissue
wrinkled as the papery skin

that wrapped them up so carefully.
Initials of long dead relatives

worn to faint memory,
one by one escaping our vocabulary.

Cut glass, always on display,
fruit dishes, brandy goblets seldom used,

facets dulled with dust
fallen like creeping years on party time.

'However old you are
you feel the same inside,'
she said.


Repeatedly.

Now I am next in line,
I say the same old things,

get out a cloth, the Duraglit
fill a soapy bowl,

unwrap the crinkled tissue
with her hands.

## Insignificance

Into the hills we climbed.
Below, striped fields lay mapped
like continents.
Sheep grazed silently,
polka-dotting summer's party frock.
Houses, matchbox small,
lanes thin as string,
hedge strands and dry-stone walls,
a toyscape, peopled with miniatures
of tractor, garden plot, and men
who, looking up, would see
almost invisible in cloud
you, me, as small, gazing across
the farness, wideness, on-ness
of it all.
Where we were going.
What we'd left behind.
What was lost, longed for, unexplained –
all one,
the shining lake,
the drowned boy on the shore,
small enough now to cover with your hand.

# Ötzi: the Iceman

## Death in the mountains

Brought down like game
a hunter dies
far from his village in an Alpine pass.
Blood from the arrow buried in his back,
blood from a head wound
crimsoning the ice.
Cold and pain slice through
his goat skin leggings
mended for longer use,
the swamp grass matting of his cloak,
the deer hide of his coat and shoes.

Earth shuts its eye on all he knew,
the flowering cloud,
the snaggleteeth of pine,
the flint stone dagger in his fist,
his long-bow leaning on the gully wall,
a bearskin hat dropped
in a mist of snow.

## His woman

Often he would be weeks away,
return with arrows gone,
a blunted axe,
the carcass of an ibex on his back.
How she would stoke the fire
in celebration, lie with him
on matting woven in long hours
from lakeside reeds,
their dwelling sweet with wood-smoke,
stews of bubbling meat and cereal.

Days rolled away from her.
She kept the hearth alive.
Lay wakeful under furs.
Buried her face in smells of him,
campfire, molten copper, grass.
Poppies reddened in the wheat,
leaked down the fields
like bloodstains to the shore.
Snow fell on the high pastures.
Arms of pine grew heavy with a weight
almost too much to bear.

He never came. Aloneness grew,
gathered around her days like moss.
The pilings of their dwelling rotted under her.
In time another took her in,
and what became of him she never knew.

Sometimes when springtime pollen shakes
from hornbeam catkins and the earth renews,
out of the broiling mist of steep and sky
she hears snow shift, earth crack,
the glacier split open like a shell.


## The villagers

The villagers wove comfort for her
out of clement weather.
'Look the sky brightens,' they would say
'the grass blows sweet,
he'll not be long away.'

'What if big snows have hindered him,
shape changed the rocks,
swallowed the sheep tracks?
He has old knowledge of The Pass,
he knows the language of the glacier,
has good shoes, good medicine,
a goatskin jerkin
warm as glowing peat.'

Or told her rumours of a mighty herd
of ibex grazing the conifers.
'He will have followed them,
your wily journeyman.
His day guide is the sun,
at night, the moon.
Arrows of wind will point him home.'

But there was one
whose heart was pitch.
Who drove his faithless woman from their hearth.
Threw the blood-stained leggings on the fire.

Knew he would not return.


## The killing

Yes I hacked off his penis and his testicles
when he was dead.
He had been warned.
Followed the randy bastard
from the valley bottom,
to the wind carved peaks.
Pursued him through the secrecy of snow.
Watched him test his axe blade with his thumb,
piss, shit, tear meat,
grow tired and slow.

He listened,
but he did not hear me come.

And yes, I smiled,
a perfect shot lined up
from far below his furtive clambering,
chose my best arrow,
drew my bow...

## Coda: September 1991

On detour in the alpine wilderness,
hikers discover on the gully floor
a mummy of a man under the ice,
shoulders and back exposed by sudden thaw.

He told them what he'd worn and how he'd died,
what food he'd eaten on that final day.
Told them his age, the colour of his eyes,
everything written in his DNA.

Not if a woman wept, if neighbours lied,
if others sowed his corn or pulled his plough.
No vestige of a thought he might have had
as snow buried a life-time. Snow. More snow.

Ötzi is a well-preserved mummy of a man who lived over 5000
years ago. He was found on September 1991 in the Ötztal Alps
on the border between Austria and Italy. His body and
belongings are displayed in the South Tyrol Museum of
Archaeology in Bolzano, South Tyrol, Italy. The exact
circumstances of his death remain unknown.

Perfume drifting back

# Flowers of The Yukon

Twinflower, Hawksbeard,
Scheuchzer's Cottongrass,
Siberian Astor, Hollow Sedge,
Foxtail Barley, Yellow Locoweed.

I can't remember where I picked them now,
what lakeside, forest clearing, gravel track,
but like uncaptioned photographs
their brittle pressings carry me
to where the Dempster's thread unspools
past blue thaw lakes, blazes of fireweed,
stunted spruce, grizzlies,
black bears and caribou.

Petals open.
Perfume drifting back.

Dempster – a 457 mile long unmade causeway over permafrost
running from the Yukon's Dawson City to Inuvik in the
Northwest Territories of Canada.

## The Yukon

This is a place where thought can grow,
here in this wilderness
of quartz striated rock,
nameless ranges crowned with snow
mirrored in lakes of rust and emerald.

Here, nothing but time and glacial history
record the contours of the world
in carbonaceous shale,
granite and dolomite.

Distance repeats itself
down ranks of raggedy black pine
hungering on the permafrost,
and in the space between
snaggles of jagged limestone teeth
silence maps out infinities of sky.

Canada geese fly shadowless.

## The Mule Deer

We chance upon a mule deer in a glade,
poised to stand ground or flee,
huge bat ears silken and erect.

Unafraid she does neither,
just eyes us suspiciously
like uninvited strangers
who have dropped into her drawing room for tea,
then tiptoes off across the shag pile grass,
retires into a private room,
closing the darkness quietly after her.

## Black Pine

I am Black Pine, my space
this thin deficient face of rock.
Each year I grow new skin,
record my history in rings.
I have no memory
but these to chart
an earlier fate.
My forest fellows imitate
my aspiration to grow tall,
fight for their little patch
of sky and soil,
assert their might.
Only our roots entwine
in networks
underground,
anchor us in such community
that when one falls
each pulls the other down.

# Grizzly

'Look for a spot on the hill,' the trapper said,
and there she was, four hundred meters off,
a brown blob quickening on the slope.
Then through the lens
up close and personal, a huge blond grizzly,
rolling like a kid in the undergrowth,
scrubbing and scratching at her winter coat,
exposing herself indelicately.
Her crazed itch-frenzy – almost comical,
a cartoon grizzly, waving her claws,
wriggling her bum in ecstasy.
It's an itch she's got to scratch
and she's overdressed for summer.

But if you go down in the woods today
and meet her face to face, speak to her softly,
say you are human, back away,
avoid her lethal manicure!

## One Moose in Two Moose Lake

She stands up to her fetlocks in the boreal lake,
pondweed hanging from her mouth like dribble.
Head of a huge donkey.
Torso a mismatch of hippo, cow and horse.
Wrestler's shoulders on her.
Nostrils you could get your fist in.

Comedy ears swivel like radar,
as we draw up for a closer look.
She clocks us with one eye
focuses the other on escape
decides against,
then ducks her big daft head
for more browse.

It's a slow, lazy business.
The water gleams with evening.
We watch her munch her cud,
placid and ruminant.

Then with a startled crystal shake
at nothing in particular
she heads for the bank,
stops to display her gorgeous racehorse legs,
pose for the camera,
then pisses One Almighty Piss –
a comment perhaps on our discourtesy?

## To Speak Beaver (for JBP)

What starts out as a pile of sticks,
becomes wet fur, becomes a beaver.

Out of some 'otherwhere' I make
a gargling chirrup, mewling call.

A cocked head pricks,
slips neck deep in the lake

pulls glimmering V's towards me
through a mirrored canopy.

I make a chirpling warble, luring coo.
Bead-bright eyes, damp dog nose

follow me curiously along the bank,
whiskers twin fans of wired light,

antennae tuned in  briefly
to a frequency we seem to share.

Then with a hump of lustrous black,
a slap of spatula, he's gone.

Since then I've watched you disappear,
your poetry, your bright intelligence,

have scanned your bandwidth
for a signal you can hear.

But ripples widen, our connection lost,
a glint of bubbles where you were.

## Caribou

A boy aged twelve,
his trapper's hat jewelled with mosquitoes,
has shot his first caribou.
We brake to investigate.

'We are Gwitch'in,' says his father,
defensive to the bone.
Five young sons shuffle from foot to foot,
study the stones.

The soft majestic head is propped
below the highway on the verge.
Glass marble eyes reflect
boreal forests, fireweed, sky,
old songs and dances, ancient tales
of herds and hunts.

We spot its severed hind-end
down the slope,
offer to help them heave it to the truck.
Job done, it's pats on the back,
first names, photographs.

This kill will feed the family for a month.

On a clear night you might see the lad
caught in a moonlit clearing at Old Crow,
alive and sacred in his hand
the heart he's sharing with the caribou.

Gwich'in means 'people of the caribou' an apt name for a First Nation people who largely rely on the caribou for food.

Caribou are an integral part of First Nation and Inuit oral histories and legends including the Gwich'in creation story of how Gwitch'in people and the caribou separated from a single entity and share the same heart.

## Eagle

Skydiver over rock. Lake.
Sun gold. Shadow.
         Silhouette.
Hangs. Soars. Makes
tears in wind. Below
         ultraviolet
mouse pee tracks
an afterglow.
         The target
meanders, shakes
tufted Cottongrass.
Nibbles.
         Silent
as a drone. Late
light. Deadly. Slow.
The raptor
         circles.
Swerves. Brakes.
Slips undertow.
Pinpoints.




         Plummets.

## Accident on The Dempster Highway

A Dormobile has nosedived
down the bank,
bumper just visible in brush.

We haven't seen a car for days,
just the odd ice-truck roaring past,
turning our windows black with grit.

We stop to help.
A door hangs open like a mouth,
tongue sticking out.

Inside a walking stick,
scattered crayons,
a colouring book.

Something on the wheel that could be blood.

Ice-trucks: huge 18-wheel trucks that carry mining material and
equipment on the dirt roads of Canada and Alaska, including
during the winter when they cross frozen lakes and rivers.

## Bear Spray

The forest was dark,
tingly with pine,
moss mounds greening
where sun lasered through
the glooming overhang.
So quiet we could hear
our collars scratch,
small twigs snap under us.

Then a louder noise,
as if a drunk was blundering
through the trees.

'Do we have the bear spray'?
I ventured in alarm.

'Bees are more dangerous than bears,'
you said,
then headed to the cabin
some way back
leaving me on the bank
to guard our bag.

Below me, through
a serried march of pine,
Lake Labarge fed quietly
on leaf mould
at the water's edge.

Silence grew loud,
a floating log grew ears
and swam.
I heard soft paw-fall
pad on cone,
a grunt, a snuffling.
A bush on hind legs
cocked and lowered its head.

I thought to address him kindly,
back into the gloom,
fade to sepia
as ghost or shadow might.
Be moss fur, fern,
the curvature of stones.

There was no bear of course,
just forest breakages,
thought print, wind lick,
root creak and water pattering.

When you returned
I was so still, so sentient,
I could hear
whispers of whiskering
mouse-breath in the grass.

Poems are on the march

## Mr Kalashnikov regrets...

If he'd known then what he knows now
how many slaughtered innocents
how many orphaned, mutilated, lamed
how many in the hands of kids who kill
how many Governments would sell
his brain-child to immoral men
how many crooked fortunes made
insurgencies sustained, illegal trade
no place beyond its muzzle's ken.
Would he do now, what he did then...?

"My spiritual pain is unbearable. I keep having the same unsolved question: if my rifle took away people's lives, then can it be that I am guilty for people's deaths, even if they were enemies?"(Mikhail Kalashnikov, inventor of the Kalashnikov automatic rifle, in a letter to The Russian Orthodox Church written shortly before his death).

## Remembrance
(On visiting The Jewish Museum, Berlin)

Remember me.
My unlived life,
lives unlived after me.

Make my unmade journey.
Sing my unsung song.
Name the future after me.
Unsay the tongues of blood,
the hiss of Zyklon B.

Write on walls of air
my testimony.
Say I was here.
I was the last.
Remember me.

Leaven me in the wilderness of loss.
Feed me on apples, cinnamon and wine.
See in the bowls of family spoons
my legacy,
the faces of my unborn line,
children unthought
before the thought was mine.

Sew me a Yellow Star to shine
on leaves, on butterflies, on skin,
stitch it in the lining of the mind.

Remember me
for all that I was not,
all that I might have been.

## Political prisoner (for GH)

They burned the scores
but not the songs he knew.

Books,
not poems written in scripts of light
inside his cage.

Photographs,
not the softness
of his mother's hands.

House,
but not homeland
built from enduring memory.

As flames grew high
spiteful as history
his captors found they'd built
a prison for themselves,
and he was free.

## Leaving Karelia 1939 (for LC)

Before The Russians
drove them from their home
their grandmother gave the baby a bath in the sauna,
grabbed coat and mittens,
buried all her precious things.
Their tears froze.

Through falling snow
they watched their village burn.

Now, far from home,
her family gather in the hearth room
on each anniversary

and they weep
for her scissors
her coffee pot

and for Karelia.

Karelian War – as a result of the 1940 Moscow Peace Treaty that concluded the Winter War, Finland ceded the area of Finnish Karelia and other territories to the Soviet Union. About 12% of Finland's population were relocated to what was left of Finland. They never went home.

## Ants

Upending a flower pot
the kids cause pandemonium.
Ants seethe a cauldron
in the root bound soil.
Alarmed and purposeless,
their careful toil
of hefting eggs,
keeping neat house,
nurturing their high queen's
progeny,
order, co-operation,
symmetry,
made chaos by this careless desecration.

The ants make random escape
over the patio ranges,
swarm over gorge of clay and root,
destroying scent trails to their provender,
and dispossessed of home and territory,
scuttle aimlessly,
salvaging what they can,
fleeing in desperate
Diaspora .

As if a bomb had fallen
on their village.

## Borders

He circles the patio.
Returns to attack
the trespasser
who fights back
with equal force.
Stunned
but fluffed up with right
they both retreat.
Return again
with mirrored might
defending territory
the width of glass.

# Letter to a soldier son (Baghdad 2003)

April 9th I write to say
'This is One Historic Day!'
The News shows scenes
of looting, jubilation, anarchy.
Iraqis throw flowers,
shout 'Long Live Bush.'
Saddam Hussein's bronze head
is booted down the alleys
of their broken city,
his toppled effigy
beaten with soles of shoes.

I Google Baghdad,
learn that the marshes of The Tigris and Euphrates
are home to pelican and stork.
That there are otters in those rivers.
Lions, wolves, gazelles are common.
Jerboas, hedgehogs, hares
have made the marshland theirs.

With all the talk of 'peace'
I find that comforting.

Chrys's son, then a Territorial Army Paratrooper, was mobilised
to Iraq in February 2003 and spent five months in action.

On April 9, 2003, the statue of Saddam Hussein was toppled in
Firdos Square by a U.S. armoured recovery vehicle, surrounded
by a celebratory group of Iraqis. Peace has not come.

## Magnolia: March 2013

my star magnolia in bud
presides in fisted beauty by the wall
bulbs in the garden
spiking through the mud
as blackbirds call
reminders of that other March
my young son packed to leave
burdened with desert camouflage
the garden bursting into leaf
my star magnolia in bud
bulbs in the garden
spiking through the mud

## The Insurrection of Poetry

Poems are on the march.
They are singing
from the rubble of Ground Zero,
the ruins of Damascus and Sarajevo,
the bomb shelters of Amiriyah,
the poisoned bodies in Halabja,
from the mouths of murdered menfolk
in Srebrenica.

Poems are growing from their winding sheets
in the mud and trenches
of butchered nature.
Their guns fire white poppies.
Their flags are the colour of rainbow.
Their hands fold paper cranes
under the olive trees.
From the bones of mutilated generations
they grow blossoms of resurrection.

Listen
you tyrants, murderers,
fundamentalist, mutilators,
rapists, occupiers,
racists, persecutors,
autocrats, crucifiers,

fanatics, torturers, liars,
obfuscators, manipulators,
warmongers,

silencers.

Listen!
Poems all over the world
are saying

ENOUGH.

الرقباء

اسمعوا!

قصائد من كل أنحاء العالم
تقول
كفى.

# The Insurrection of Poetry

(Arabic translation by Iraqi poet Ghareeb Iskander).

تمرد الشعر

القصائد تسير قدماً
وتغني
من تحت أنقاض غراوند زيرو
خرائب دمشق وسراييفو
قنابل ملجأ العامرية
الأجساد المتسممة بحلبجة
من أفواه الرجال القتلى
بسريبرينيتشا

القصائد تنمو من صفحاتها المطوية
في وحل وخنادق
الطبيعة المذبوحة.

بنادقهم تطلق خشخاشاً أبيض.
ألوان راياتهم تتلون بألوان قوس قزح.
أياديهم تطوي سقالات من الأوراق
تحت أشجار الزيتون.
من عظام الأجيال المشوهة
تنمو أزهار القيامة

اسمعوا
أيها الطغاة، القتلة،
المتشددون، المشوِهون
المغتصبون، المحتلون،
العنصريون، المضطهدون،
المستبدون، الجلادون
المتعصبون، المعذِبون، الكذابون،
الظلاميون، المتلاعبون،
دعاة الحرب

# Reel Iraq: March 2013

For Ghareeb Iskander, Zahir Mousa and Awezan Nury.


Zahir lost his luggage so he wears
my husband's woolly hat.
He seems perplexed by my egg-cup,
he likes his eggs hard boiled,
eats them like apples.

We light a Chinese lantern for Awezan,
release it from the patio under icy stars.
Today is her daughter's fourteenth Birthday,
and the Kurdish New Year.

Joy is not lost in translation.

Nothing and everything is understood.

Ghareeb and I swap email numbers.
Books of our poetry.

The sky was pale as shell.
Snow upon snow unmade our garden
when they came,
but under it, all March's yellow daffodils.

Too long has war unmade their land.
Now I'll try eggs the Iraqi way.

Reel Iraq was a Festival to mark the 10th Anniversary of the military invasion of Iraq. Three Iraqi poets read their work with poets from across the UK. Chrys was privileged to be one of those poets and is now working with Ghareeb Iskander on cross-translations of their work.

## Dancing on a Rock

I hear it in dark corners
lit by words
in insects stirring before gossamer
in din of arguments
in print interred
high song of larks
low syllables of home.

I hear it when night bends round sleep
and waking finds it finished
round and true
in nakedness
forked tongues
old mysteries
in silences that speak
batter of guns and bombs
making unmaking making all anew.

I hear it when feet crunch on hope
in exits entrances and loss
bombed houses
dying children
journeys to and fro
messages in spidery scrawl
coded uncoded
left behind
in burnt out rooms
charred paper scraps

the leavings in a bowl.

I hear it in vacancy
in monuments
knees scraping on lost histories
in rotting garbage
choirs in stalls
dust fall
dark passages
brush stroke
gilt glint
unwritten maps
antiquities.

I hear it in the death of bees
beginnings
endings
running in and out
weigh it with hair
count it with petal fall

in a fossil dancing on a rock
hear it in everything
after
before
and after all of this.

Indigo Dreams Publishing Ltd
24, Forest Houses
Cookworthy Moor
Halwill
Beaworthy
Devon
EX21 5UU
www.indigodreams.co.uk